BRIAN BURGESS

We Will See Our Pets In Heaven

THE AFTERLIFE OF ANIMALS
FROM A BIBLICAL PERSPECTIVE

outskirtspress
DENVER, COLORADO

The opinions expressed in this manuscript are solely the opinions of the author and do not represent the opinions or thoughts of the publisher. The author has represented and warranted full ownership and/or legal right to publish all the materials in this book.

We Will See Our Pets In Heaven
The Afterlife of Animals from a Biblical Perspective
All Rights Reserved.
Copyright © 2013 Brian Burgess
v3.0 r1.1

All Scripture references taken from the PC Study Bible.

Cover Photo © 2013 JupiterImages Corporation. All rights reserved - used with permission.

This book may not be reproduced, transmitted, or stored in whole or in part by any means, including graphic, electronic, or mechanical without the express written consent of the publisher except in the case of brief quotations embodied in critical articles and reviews.

Outskirts Press, Inc.
http://www.outskirtspress.com

ISBN: 978-1-4787-1697-6

Outskirts Press and the "OP" logo are trademarks belonging to Outskirts Press, Inc.

PRINTED IN THE UNITED STATES OF AMERICA

Dedicated to Luke and Sarah

In Loving Memory

Ps 36:6
*6 Your righteousness is like the mountains of God;
your judgments are like the great deep;
man and beast you save, O Lord.*

∽∽

"If there are no dogs in Heaven, then when I die I want to go where they went."

– Will Rogers

Contents

Introduction i
Where Does It Say 1
The Fall 3
They Had to Die for Us 7
Our Future Glory 9
What Does God Think About Our Relationship
   with Our Animals 14
God Cares For and Loves His Animals 17
His Creatures Praise Him 24
Commonly Misinterpreted Verses 27
Forever 42
Proof There Are Animals in Heaven Right Now 44
Will We Remember Our Pets?
   Will They Remember Us? 46
Reality of Heaven 61
The Good News 68
Do You Know What It Takes to Get to Heaven 69
Reading List 73

Introduction

The subject of whether we will see our pets in heaven has been sorely neglected far too long. The reason I say this is because I have heard many people throughout the years make disparaging comments about animals not going to heaven based on various assumptions and misinterpreted bible verses. It hurts when you lose a pet. I know. And it doesn't help the grieving process when people say they are gone forever, or they are just animals, that they don't have souls etc. Although there have been books written on the subject I feel that more awareness is still needed in this area. I have had many pets throughout the years and it always hurts when I have to say goodbye. In this book I show that there is much biblical evidence that animals do indeed go to heaven. I was inspired to write this book after losing my Black Lab to old age. We raised her from a puppy and she lived 13 years 5 months. She passed away in December 2009. In May 2011 my Golden Retriever passed away. We also raised him from a puppy. He was

13 years 2 months. Both dogs were very much loved and part of the family. Most people who have ever had a pet, know the bond that can develop over time and the unconditional love that is shared. Our pets become part of the family. They are considered much more than just dogs or cats or rabbits etc. We love them and they love us. I have had many pets through the years and every time one dies I feel like a part of me dies with them. The thought that I would never see them again prompted me to look in to this subject more deeply and get a biblical perspective of whether or not we would see our pets again……..I believe we will!

Where Does It Say

There is no single passage in the bible that says conclusively that our pets will go to heaven, however, there is much biblical evidence that gives us much hope that they will be there.

When God created the heavens and the earth, it was not his intention that any of his creation would suffer death and decay. That includes the animals. Another interesting point I would like to mention at this time is that God created the animals before he created man and he was pleased with his creation.

Gen 1:25-26
25 And God made the beasts of the earth according to their kinds and the livestock according to their kinds, and everything that creeps on the ground according to its kind. And God saw that it was good.

26 Then God said, "Let us make man in our image, after our likeness. And let them have dominion over the fish of the sea and over the birds of the heavens and over the livestock and over all the earth and over every creeping thing that creeps on the earth."
ESV

Just something to think about. Also, it was never Gods intention that we would eat any of his animals.

Gen 1:29-30
29 And God said, "Behold, I have given you every plant yielding seed that is on the face of all the earth, and every tree with seed in its fruit. You shall have them for food.

30 And to every beast of the earth and to every bird of the heavens and to everything that creeps on the earth, everything that has the breath of life, I have given every green plant for food." And it was so.
ESV

Again in *Genesis 1: 31*, God saw everything that he made and it was very good.

Gen 1:31
31 And God saw everything that he had made, and behold, it was very good. And there was evening and there was morning, the sixth day.
ESV

The Fall

It was not until after Adam and Eve sinned that God cursed the earth and we are still living under that curse today. In *Genesis 2: 17*, Gods instruction to Adam was not to eat of the tree of the knowledge of good and evil lest he should die.

Gen 2:17
17 but of the tree of the knowledge of good and evil you shall not eat, for in the day that you eat of it you shall surely die."
ESV

As the story goes according to chapter 3, Eve was deceived by the serpent and ate the forbidden fruit and gave to Adam to eat also. Clearly we can see from this passage of scripture, why we and the animals that God put in subjection to us suffer death today.

WE WILL SEE OUR PETS IN HEAVEN

Gen 3:1-6
1 Now the serpent was more crafty than any other beast of the field that the Lord God had made. He said to the woman, "Did God actually say, 'You shall not eat of any tree in the garden'?"

2 And the woman said to the serpent, "We may eat of the fruit of the trees in the garden,

3 but God said, 'You shall not eat of the fruit of the tree that is in the midst of the garden, neither shall you touch it, lest you die.'"

4 But the serpent said to the woman, "You will not surely die.

5 For God knows that when you eat of it your eyes will be opened, and you will be like God, knowing good and evil."

6 So when the woman saw that the tree was good for food, and that it was a delight to the eyes, and that the tree was to be desired to make one wise, she took of its fruit and ate, and she also gave some to her husband who was with her, and he ate.
ESV

When God told Adam that he would die if he ate of the tree of the knowledge of good and evil, he wasn't lying. It was Satan that lied. When Adam and Eve ate

THE FALL

the forbidden fruit they may have died instantly in a spiritual sense in that they were separated from God by their sin, but obviously God also meant they would die physically even though their physical death didn't come till much later.

Gen 3:8-19
8 And they heard the sound of the Lord God walking in the garden in the cool of the day, and the man and his wife hid themselves from the presence of the Lord God among the trees of the garden.

9 But the Lord God called to the man and said to him, "Where are you?"

10 And he said, "I heard the sound of you in the garden, and I was afraid, because I was naked, and I hid myself."

11 He said, "Who told you that you were naked? Have you eaten of the tree of which I commanded you not to eat?"

12 The man said, "The woman whom you gave to be with me, she gave me fruit of the tree, and I ate."

13 Then the Lord God said to the woman, "What is this that you have done?" The woman said, "The serpent deceived me, and I ate."

14 The Lord God said to the serpent, "Because you have

done this, cursed are you above all livestock and above all beasts of the field; on your belly you shall go, and dust you shall eat all the days of your life.

15 I will put enmity between you and the woman, and between your offspring and her offspring; he shall bruise your head, and you shall bruise his heel."

16 To the woman he said, "I will surely multiply your pain in childbearing; in pain you shall bring forth children. Your desire shall be for your husband, and he shall rule over you."

17 And to Adam he said, "Because you have listened to the voice of your wife and have eaten of the tree of which I commanded you, 'You shall not eat of it,' cursed is the ground because of you; in pain you shall eat of it all the days of your life;

18 thorns and thistles it shall bring forth for you; and you shall eat the plants of the field.

19 By the sweat of your face you shall eat bread, till you return to the ground, for out of it you were taken; for you are dust, and to dust you shall return."
ESV

They Had to Die for Us

Since God put the innocent animals under our subjection, *Genesis 1:26* they had to die also even though they did nothing wrong. They are sinless. Can you imagine what it would be like if God exempted the animals from suffering death. With all the evil and cruelty in the world today because of mans sin I would feel sorry for the animals if they had to endlessly endure the wickedness of this world until Jesus returns. I think that it is God's mercy that he has shortened their lives here on earth so they wouldn't have to. They are indeed a blessing from God and it is very painful when we have to say goodbye. If anyone deserves to go to heaven it is the animals simply because they are the innocent ones, not us. The blood of innocent animals was even shed for the atonement of our sins before Jesus came as we can see throughout Old Testament history; however, it was not enough. It took the shed blood of God's only son Jesus Christ as the perfect atonement for our sins, thus ending animal sacrifices altogether.

WE WILL SEE OUR PETS IN HEAVEN

Heb 9:11-14
11 But when Christ appeared as a high priest of the good things that have come, then through the greater and more perfect tent (not made with hands, that is, not of this creation)

12 he entered once for all into the holy places, not by means of the blood of goats and calves but by means of his own blood, thus securing an eternal redemption.

13 For if the sprinkling of defiled persons with the blood of goats and bulls and with the ashes of a heifer sanctifies for the purification of the flesh,

14 how much more will the blood of Christ, who through the eternal Spirit offered himself without blemish to God, purify our conscience from dead works to serve the living God.
ESV

Our Future Glory

Doesn't it stand to reason then, that if God never intended us, or the animals, to die in the beginning, and it was because of the sin of Adam and Eve, that God cursed the earth, that God will allow his animals to go to heaven and even be resurrected with the rest of us when Jesus returns? Consider the following verses.

Rom 8:18-23
18 For I consider that the sufferings of this present time are not worth comparing with the glory that is to be revealed to us.

19 For the creation waits with eager longing for the revealing of the sons of God.

20 For the creation was subjected to futility, not willingly, but because of him who subjected it, in hope

21 that the creation itself will be set free from its bondage to decay and obtain the freedom of the glory of the children of God.

22 For we know that the whole creation has been groaning together in the pains of childbirth until now.

23 And not only the creation, but we ourselves, who have the firstfruits of the Spirit, groan inwardly as we wait eagerly for adoption as sons, the redemption of our bodies. ESV

Rev 21:1-5
1 Then I saw a new heaven and a new earth, for the first heaven and the first earth had passed away, and the sea was no more.

2 And I saw the holy city, new Jerusalem, coming down out of heaven from God, prepared as a bride adorned for her husband.

3 And I heard a loud voice from the throne saying, "Behold, the dwelling place of God is with man. He will dwell with them, and they will be his people, and God himself will be with them as their God.

4 He will wipe away every tear from their eyes, and death shall be no more, neither shall there be mourning nor crying nor pain anymore, for the former things have passed away."

OUR FUTURE GLORY

5 And he who was seated on the throne said, "Behold, I am making all things new." Also he said, "Write this down, for these words are trustworthy and true."
ESV

Clearly we can see from just these few passages alone, that the time will come when God will restore his creation to its former glory where there will be no more suffering or death. Imagine that, a new heaven and a new earth. Not a different heaven and earth that is new but this heaven and earth *made* new. Take a closer look at *Rev 21:5*. It says, "Behold, I am making all things new." Not "I am making all new things." Also, *Rom 8:19-21* clearly show that it's this creation that is now waiting, and will someday, be set free from its bondage of decay to obtain the freedom of the glory of the children of God. Look at *Eph 1:9-10*. The time will come when all things will be united in him, things in heaven and things on earth.

Eph 1:9-10
9 making known to us the mystery of his will, according to his purpose, which he set forth in Christ

10 as a plan for the fullness of time, to unite all things in him, things in heaven and things on earth.
ESV

Also, look what the apostle Paul says about the resurrection in *1 Cor 15:35-44*, especially verse 44. <u>*If there is a natural body, there is also a spiritual body.*</u>

1 Cor 15:35-44
35 But someone will ask, "How are the dead raised? With what kind of body do they come?"

36 You foolish person! What you sow does not come to life unless it dies.

37 And what you sow is not the body that is to be, but a bare kernel, perhaps of wheat or of some other grain.

38 But God gives it a body as he has chosen, and to each kind of seed its own body.

39 For not all flesh is the same, but there is one kind for humans, another for animals, another for birds, and another for fish.

40 There are heavenly bodies and earthly bodies, but the glory of the heavenly is of one kind, and the glory of the earthly is of another.

41 There is one glory of the sun, and another glory of the moon, and another glory of the stars; for star differs from star in glory.

OUR FUTURE GLORY

42 So is it with the resurrection of the dead. What is sown is perishable; what is raised is imperishable.

43 It is sown in dishonor; it is raised in glory. It is sown in weakness; it is raised in power.

44 It is sown a natural body; it is raised a spiritual body. If there is a natural body, there is also a spiritual body.
<u>*ESV*</u>

What Does God Think About Our Relationship with Our Animals

So what does God think about our relationship with animals? In *2 Sam :12* God sends Nathan the prophet to David because David did evil in the sight of the Lord by sending Uriah the Hittite to the front line in battle so that he could be struck down by the Ammonites. With Uriah out of the way, David was then able to marry Uriah's wife who he lusted after. This act by David displeased the Lord so the Lord sent Nathan the prophet to David so that Nathan could point out his transgression. Let's see what Nathan said.

2 Sam 12:1-9
1 And the Lord sent Nathan to David. He came to him and said to him, "There were two men in a certain city, the one rich and the other poor.

2 The rich man had very many flocks and herds,

WHAT DOES GOD THINK...

3 but the poor man had nothing but one little ewe lamb, which he had bought. And he brought it up, and it grew up with him and with his children. It used to eat of his morsel and drink from his cup and lie in his arms, and it was like a daughter to him.

4 Now there came a traveler to the rich man, and he was unwilling to take one of his own flock or herd to prepare for the guest who had come to him, but he took the poor man's lamb and prepared it for the man who had come to him."

5 Then David's anger was greatly kindled against the man, and he said to Nathan, "As the Lord lives, the man who has done this deserves to die,

6 and he shall restore the lamb fourfold, because he did this thing, and because he had no pity."

7 Nathan said to David, "You are the man! Thus says the Lord, the God of Israel, 'I anointed you king over Israel, and I delivered you out of the hand of Saul.

8 And I gave you your master's house and your master's wives into your arms and gave you the house of Israel and of Judah. And if this were too little, I would add to you as much more.

9 Why have you despised the word of the Lord, to do what is evil in his sight? You have struck down Uriah the Hittite

WE WILL SEE OUR PETS IN HEAVEN

with the sword and have taken his wife to be your wife and have killed him with the sword of the Ammonites.
ESV

Isn't it interesting how Nathan used the story of a man and his pet lamb to show David the evil he was guilty of? Judging from verse 5, even David himself was angry at the man in Nathans story. Do you think God would have allowed Nathan to use such a story about a man and his pet lamb if there was anything unnatural or evil about the bond that can develop between man and animal? I don't think so. If anything, Nathans story shows me that not only does God understand the relationship and bond and love that can develop between man and animal, he also approves of it or else he would not have allowed Nathan to use such an illustration to show David the evil he was guilty of. Could we not only conclude from these passages then, that if we are faithful Christians, when we get to heaven our pets will be waiting for us there? I believe so.

God Cares For and Loves His Animals

According to *Matt 10:29-30* and *Luke 12:6,* not one little sparrow is forgotten before God or falls to the ground without his knowledge. So what message do you suppose Jesus is trying to convey with these verses? Read *Matt 10: 26-33* and *Luke 12:4-7.*

Matt 10:26-33
26 "So have no fear of them, for nothing is covered that will not be revealed, or hidden that will not be known.

27 What I tell you in the dark, say in the light, and what you hear whispered, proclaim on the housetops.

28 And do not fear those who kill the body but cannot kill the soul. Rather fear him who can destroy both soul and body in hell.

WE WILL SEE OUR PETS IN HEAVEN

29 Are not two sparrows sold for a penny? And not one of them will fall to the ground apart from your Father.

30 But even the hairs of your head are all numbered.

31 Fear not, therefore; you are of more value than many sparrows.

32 So everyone who acknowledges me before men, I also will acknowledge before my Father who is in heaven,

33 but whoever denies me before men, I also will deny before my Father who is in heaven.
ESV

Luke 12:4-7
4 "I tell you, my friends, do not fear those who kill the body, and after that have nothing more that they can do.

5 But I will warn you whom to fear: fear him who, after he has killed, has authority to cast into hell. Yes, I tell you, fear him!

6 Are not five sparrows sold for two pennies? And not one of them is forgotten before God.

7 Why, even the hairs of your head are all numbered. Fear not; you are of more value than many sparrows.
ESV

GOD CARES FOR AND LOVES HIS ANIMALS

What Jesus is saying here is for us to be of good courage and have no fear of people who may persecute you in one form or another for confessing him (Jesus) as Lord. He mentions specifically men "killing the body" which we do not have to be too concerned about in this country but we also need to be bold enough to not let ridicule hinder us from acknowledging Jesus as our Savior also. He goes on to say that whoever acknowledges him before men, he will acknowledge to our father in heaven, and that we are of much more value than many sparrows. Isn't it interesting though how he compares our value to an insignificant little sparrow? We see those little birds everyday yet for the most part do not give them a second thought, but God does, according to these verses. Not one little sparrow is forgotten or falls to the ground apart from our father in heaven. Now just think about that for a moment. We can see from these verses that we are of much more value than an insignificant little sparrow yet God still places enough value on them that not one is forgotten or falls to the ground without his knowledge. Now let's just clarify right now what he means when he uses the phrase "falls to the ground." Very simply it means that the creature dies a physical death. Sparrows do not just fall to the ground unless they are dead. Simple fact. Judging from these 2 verses alone then, do you think that little sparrow that falls to the ground is going to be annihilated or cease to exist. Does it make sense that God would allow them to be annihilated or cease to exist if they are "not forgotten" as it says in *Luke 12:6*? I should say not! If God doesn't forget them when they fall to the ground, would it make any sense then to conclude that they would cease to exist when they fell to the ground. If they were to cease to exist when they fell to the ground then couldn't God just as easily forget about them then if they're going to be gone forever? Do you see what I'm getting at? So what am I saying then? Does every little sparrow that falls to the ground go to heaven? Yes! That is exactly what I'm saying! God doesn't forget them as we've just seen and that goes for every creature that has the breath of life. If it's true for the insignificant little sparrow as we've just read then the only logical conclusion is that the same holds true for all of God's creatures, and that also includes our pets that we hold so dear to our hearts. According to *Ps:24:1, Ps:50:10-11,* the earth and all creatures belong to him, and again we see in *Ps 104:10-13, Ps 145:9,15-17, Ps 147:9,* how much he cares for his creatures, how righteous our Heavenly Father is and how all his creatures look to him for sustenance.

Ps 24:1
24 The earth is the Lord's and the fullness thereof, the world and those who dwell therein,
ESV

Ps 50:10-11
10 For every beast of the forest is mine, the cattle on a thousand hills.

GOD CARES FOR AND LOVES HIS ANIMALS

11 I know all the birds of the hills, and all that moves in the field is mine.
ESV

Ps 104:10-13
10 You make springs gush forth in the valleys; they flow between the hills;

11 they give drink to every beast of the field; the wild donkeys quench their thirst.

12 Beside them the birds of the heavens dwell; they sing among the branches.
ESV

13 From your lofty abode you water the mountains; the earth is satisfied with the fruit of your work.
ESV

Ps 145:9,15-17
9 He gives to the beasts their food, and to the young ravens that cry.

15 The eyes of all look to you, and you give them their food in due season.

16 You open your hand; you satisfy the desire of every living thing.

17 The Lord is righteous in all his ways and kind in all his works.
ESV

Ps 147:9
9 He gives to the beasts their food, and to the young ravens that cry.
ESV

Not only does God care for his creatures, we humans are expected to care for them also according to *Proverbs 12:10*.

Prov 12:10
10 Whoever is righteous has regard for the life of his beast, but the mercy of the wicked is cruel.
ESV

When I look at *Prov 12:10* I can't help but think about the needless suffering animals go through at science laboratories, at the hands of uncompassionate owners and the ruthless child who doesn't know any better. I personally would rather die than benefit from any medical advances made at the expense of an animal that had to suffer. I won't mention the atrocities and cruelty those poor animals have to endure at the hands of the so called scientists at medical and research laboratories because it is just to graphic. I have read about some of what goes on and it's very sad and heartbreaking. The

GOD CARES FOR AND LOVES HIS ANIMALS

people that subject those animals to such pain and suffering are indeed the wicked the writer is referring to in this passage of scripture and when they stand before God in judgment they are going to get what's coming to them.

His Creatures Praise Him

You'll also be amazed to know that his creatures praise him according to *Ps 150:6* and *Rev 5:13*.

Ps 150:6
6 Let everything that has breath praise the Lord! Praise the Lord!
ESV

Rev 5:13
13 And I heard every creature in heaven and on earth and under the earth and in the sea, and all that is in them, saying, "To him who sits on the throne and to the Lamb be blessing and honor and glory and might forever and ever!"
ESV

We can only speculate how exactly his creatures praise him but the important thing here is the fact that they do. Perhaps they praise him by just being who they are and the fact they exist and declare our Heavenly Father's incredible design and handiwork much the way a painting reflects an artist's talent and ability. Maybe there is a certain sound they make that may of course not make any sense to us or maybe it's a sound that we as humans cannot even hear. According to *Rev 5:13-14* they are actual spoken words, however much of the book of Revelation is figurative, the message, nevertheless, is that every creature is praising our heavenly father, however it is not entirely impossible for an animal to speak words that we can understand. I'll talk about that in a moment. Have you ever wondered what it would be like if you could communicate with your pet? We already communicate with our pets but on an extremely limited basis. We can teach them basic commands, which they respond to by the sound of different words like no, come, sit, stay, and the list could go on and on, and they communicate with us by certain behaviors or a particular sound depending on the kind of pet you have. My dogs let me know when they want to go out by standing by the door and making certain sounds. Then they let me know when they want to come in by scratching at the door and making a high pitch bark. When they want a biscuit they go stand by the pantry and make a kind of whining sound. They make yet a different sounding kind of bark when someone's outside and even different sounds when they want to play or be petted and the list goes on. You get my point. But when we get to heaven and are reunited with our pets, and we are no longer under the curse as we have seen spoken of in Genesis, it is quite possible that we will be able to talk with our pets and they will be able to talk to us and I'll tell you why. Read *Gen: 3* where Eve is having a conversation with the serpent and *Num 22:28-30* concerning the conversation Balaam was having with his donkey. Notice anything strange about their conversation. Neither Eve nor Balaam seemed to be the least bit shocked, surprised or alarmed that they were talking to creatures other than humans. It must have been at one time that it may have been commonplace for animals to be able to talk to humans using actual words that we understand.

Num 22:28-30
28 Then the Lord opened the mouth of the donkey, and she said to Balaam, "What have I done to you, that you have struck me these three times?"

29 And Balaam said to the donkey, "Because you have made a fool of me. I wish I had a sword in my hand, for then I would kill you."

30 And the donkey said to Balaam, "Am I not your donkey, on which you have ridden all your life long to this day? Is it my habit to treat you this way?"
ESV

Commonly Misinterpreted Verses

I would like to dispel the idea that some people have that animals don't go to heaven based on certain bible passages and the idea that animals do not have a soul. Five bible verses that I know of that many people misinterpret are as follows:

1. *Eccl 3:21*
   21. Who knows whether the spirit of man goes upward and the spirit of the beast goes down into the earth?
   ESV

This verse is posed as a question. The preacher here doesn't know whether the spirit of the beast goes up or down, but in light of what we know so far what the bible says about animals and how much God cares for them and loves them, can't we conclude then that the spirit of the animal would go up to be with the

Lord and those who cared for and loved them in this life? Not only that but we can also conclude from this verse (as well as many others not yet mentioned) that animals do indeed have a spirit, *(1 Cor 15:44)* and it is not destroyed, annihilated, does not disappear or cease to exist when the physical body dies but clearly goes somewhere. And I believe that "somewhere" is heaven and not down to the earth as the preacher poses the question. As far as whether they have a soul or not, to me that question is a no brainer. Of course they have a soul. It is different from our soul because we were made in the image of God. That is, we have self awareness, the ability to reason. Animals do not. At least not to the extent that we humans have. Our soul is who we are. It is our personality, our likes and dislikes, everything we have experienced in this life from our birth that has influenced who we are today. It is the same with animals. They have personalities, likes and dislikes, and are also capable of feeling many of the same emotions that we as humans experience. Just look at their body language throughout the day. See how happy they are when you give them a treat for example, take them for a walk, play with them or invite them to sit beside you on the sofa. If you have ever raised a puppy you can see the changes in their personality as they grow up and they learn right from wrong. If you have ever owned and cared for a pet you must know this from firsthand experience. Like for example when you have to leave for work in the morning your pet may show signs of depression or sadness.

COMMONLY MISINTERPRETED VERSES

My dogs would just lie on the floor or sofa, motionless and quite subdued looking up at me as I pet them and say goodbye when I have to leave for work or some other activity. Sometimes they would even wait for me by the door thinking that I was going to take them for a walk. They love going for walks. You can see the happiness in them by their wagging tails and overall body language. The same can be said when you are teaching them right from wrong, for example telling them no and refraining them from getting in to the trash or eating the cat food. They can be just like children sometimes because they will try to get away with things when they know it is wrong. Our black lab Sarah who passed away in Dec 2009 use to take dishes out of the dishwasher as we were loading it and run away with a plate or fork or whatever she could get her mouth on so she could lick whatever food morsels were left. When we caught up with her to take whatever she had out of her mouth she would sheepishly look up at you with those sad brown eyes and drop whatever she had in her mouth. She use to love to snuggle up with pillows. When she was a puppy many times she would grab a shoe or some article of clothing, maybe a magazine or even a dish left out that didn't make it to the sink, whatever might be lying around, and bring it to my wife or myself, dropping it in our laps, wagging her tail, happy as can be as though to say, look what I brought you! A present! Her and Luke our Golden Retriever who passed away in May 2011 both loved the water. The difference was that Luke use to like to play in and lie in the little kitty pool we had in our back yard whereas Sarah didn't care for that at all. She preferred the creek where we use to stop sometimes on our walks. Now Luke didn't like the creek. He would only wade in for a moment or so to get his feet wet and he was out. Luke use to always love to play with the water hose too whereas Sarah did not. Anytime I had the sprinkler running or was watering the shrubs he would be right there trying to catch the stream in his mouth. Both of them also loved the snow but especially Luke. When the snow was deep he would play for hours running around and burrowing his head in it. I use to rake the snow off the roof to prevent roof dams and he would be right there under the edge of the roof so the snow would fall on him. We always gave our dogs and cats tremendous love and they returned that love many times. Since the passing of Luke and Sarah we have since adopted two more dogs from the local animal shelter. Both very loving dogs. Buddy who is a mix, possibly lab and retriever and Beardsley. Beardsley is a very interesting looking dog. And very sassy. The people at the shelter thought maybe he was a black lab terrier mix but when we took him to the vet they had their doubts and offered a free DNA test. He is actually half German Wire Hair Pointer, quarter German Sheppard and quarter mixed breed. One thing he likes to do is take things that he knows he isn't suppose to have and make you chase him around to get it back. When he wants a bone or food or the other dog has something he wants or you tell him no he really puts up a fuss. He makes more sounds than any other dog I've ever had and very defiant. But, like I said, he is a very loving dog. He loves attention and loves to snuggle with us when we go to bed at night and sits with us on the sofa. He loves to be petted a lot also and when he wants you to pet him he definitely lets you know. He was only about six months old when we got him and boy was he a hand full. We got Luke and Sarah shortly after they were weaned and they were quite a handful too but nothing quite like Beardsley. Buddy on the other hand was about 8 years when we got him. Very docile and at times quite timid. I guess we'll never know how his previous owners treated him but I'll guess it probably wasn't the best. I think he must have been beaten because one night when we came home as soon as I opened the door I could smell poop. Beardsley was in his pen because he was still too young and very destructive to be left alone. But poor ole Buddy. I guess he was just nervous from being in a strange place and then being left alone, he had an accident and was trying to hide under the kitchen table. After talking to him and petting him and giving him lots of love he finally came out. I could tell you many, many stories of all the dogs and cats I've had the pleasure to care for over the years and their funny antics.

Anyway, the point I'm trying to make here is that animals do have souls. According to Nelsons Bible

Dictionary the word "Soul" has 2 distinct meanings but pay close attention to the second meaning.

SOUL

1. That which makes a human or animal body alive. This usage of the word soul refers to life in the physical body. The best example of this usage are those passages in the New Testament in which the Greek word for soul is translated as life. "For whoever desires to save his life [soul] will lose it," Jesus declared, "but whoever loses his life [soul] for My sake and the gospel's will save it. For what will it profit a man if he gains the whole world, and loses his own soul?" (Mark 8:36-37). This idea is also present in the Old Testament. For example, the soul of a dying person departed at death (Gen 35:18). The prophet Elijah brought a child back to life by stretching himself upon the child three times and praying that God would let the child's soul come back into him (1 Kings 17:19-23).

2. The word soul also refers to the inner life of man, the seat of his emotions, and the center of human personality. The first use of the word soul in the Old Testament expresses this meaning: "And the Lord God formed man of the dust of the ground, and breathed into his nostrils the breath of life; and man became a living being (soul)" (Gen 2:7).

COMMONLY MISINTERPRETED VERSES

This means more than being given physical life; the biblical writer declares that man became a "living soul," or a person, a human being, one distinct from all other animals. The soul is described as the seat of many emotions and desires: the desire for food (Deut 12:20-21), love (Song 1:7), longing for God (Ps 63:1), rejoicing (Ps 86:4), knowing (Ps 139:14), and memory (Lam 3:20). In the New Testament, Jesus spoke of his soul as being "exceedingly sorrowful" (Matt 26:38). Mary, the mother of Jesus, proclaimed that her soul "magnifies the Lord" (Luke 1:46). John prayed that Gaius would "prosper in all things and be in health, just as your soul prospers" (3 John 2).

(from Nelson's Illustrated Bible Dictionary, Copyright © 1986, Thomas Nelson Publishers)

So, according to the second definition, if the soul is the part of us that is our personality that makes up who we are, then it must be that animals have souls since they all have their own personalities that make up who they are but like I said before, their souls are different from our souls because we were made in the image of God.

Gen 1:26-27
26 Then God said, "Let us make man in our image, after our likeness. And let them have dominion over the fish of the sea and over the birds of the heavens and over the

livestock and over all the earth and over every creeping thing that creeps on the earth."

27 So God created man in his own image, in the image of God he created him; male and female he created them.
ESV

But let's just say for the sake of argument that they didn't have souls as some people believe. Can you deny that they are still living beings that have feelings, emotions, and personalities? And since God made them to begin with, could not God also give them a spiritual body in heaven and resurrect them again when the time comes. Remember what the apostle Paul said about the resurrection of the dead in *1 Cor 15:35-44?* God can do anything! And I believe he will since he made them, he loves them, he loved them before we did since he made them and he never intended them to die to begin with. Keep this in mind also. God loves us. He knows we love our pets. Why wouldn't he allow us to have their companionship in heaven?

Jer 32:27
27. "Behold, I am the Lord, the God of __all flesh__. Is anything too hard for me?
ESV

COMMONLY MISINTERPRETED VERSES

2. Ps 49:10-12
10 For he sees that even the wise die; the fool and the stupid alike must perish and leave their wealth to others.

11 Their graves are their homes forever, their dwelling places to all generations, though they called lands by their own names.

12 Man in his pomp will not remain; he is like the beasts that perish.
ESV

Some people take *Psalm 49:12* completely out of context to try to prove that animals won't go to heaven, but look at verses 10 and 11. The writer here is comparing foolish and stupid men, who do not worship our heavenly father nor regard him with the fear and reverence he deserves, but instead live sinful selfish lives hoarding all the wealth they can, eventually dying, their flesh and bones returning to dust, and all the wealth they ever accumulated being taken over by others, with wise men, who did put God first in their lives, and beasts. Consider how a beast *(or animal)* comes into the world compared to man. Both are conceived, there is a gestation period, and we are born with not so much as a stitch of clothes on our back. We live our lives and we die. Just like an animal.

3. *Eccl 3:19-20*
   19 For what happens to the children of man and what happens to the beasts is the same; as one dies, so dies the other. They all have the same breath, and man has no advantage over the beasts, for all is vanity.

   20 All go to one place. All are from the dust, and to dust all return.
   ESV

Any material wealth we accumulate in this life means nothing. The message here is not to be selfish and put so much value and importance on material things, because just like the wise man and the animal, we are all going to return to the dust. Put God first in your life. Lay up for yourself treasures in heaven, not on earth.

Matt 6:19-21
19 "Do not lay up for yourselves treasures on earth, where moth and rust destroy and where thieves break in and steal,

20 but lay up for yourselves treasures in heaven, where neither moth nor rust destroys and where thieves do not break in and steal.

21 For where your treasure is, there your heart will be also.
ESV

COMMONLY MISINTERPRETED VERSES

1 John 2:17
17 And the world is passing away along with its desires, but whoever does the will of God abides forever.
ESV

There is nothing wrong with being wealthy as long as you keep God first place, do what God wants you to do. Don't let wealth and worldly things become your idol. In no way do these verses say anything about anybody going to hell, ceasing to exist or becoming annihilated. These verses are merely pointing out the futility of amassing fortunes in this life whether you are a fool, stupid or wise. Now, we can reason among ourselves that the foolish and stupid person, by definition, is not going to heaven because they disobeyed God and did not put him first in their lives and there are plenty of Bible passages to support this reasoning.

4. 2 Peter 2:12
   12 But these, like irrational animals, creatures of instinct, born to be caught and destroyed, blaspheming about matters of which they are ignorant, will also be destroyed in their destruction
   ESV

5. Jude 1:10
   10 But these people blaspheme all that they do not understand, and they are destroyed by all that they, like unreasoning animals, understand instinctively.
   ESV

In order to gain full understanding of the previous verses you really need to read the full 2nd chapter of 2 Peter and the entire book of Jude. The authors of the previous passages are warning the church against false teachers and the dangers of them gaining influence and leading Christians away from the gospel and they are using animals to compare them to. As we are quite aware, animals are not made in God's image, hence, they are creatures of instinct, unable to reason, unlike us humans who were created in Gods image, we are creatures of reason and intellect, as stated in *Genesis 1:26*. The thing that separates us from the animals, of course, is our superior intellect, our ability to make rational decisions. Now let us consider the type of animal that Peter uses to compare with the false teacher. "*Creatures of instinct, born to be caught and destroyed*". Now we know, according to *Genesis 1:25* that God did not create any animals solely for the purpose of being caught and destroyed. According to *Genesis 1:25* after God created the animals, he saw that it was good. If what he created was good then why would he want them destroyed? After God created all the animals and saw that it was good, do you think he meant they were good animals to be caught and destroyed? That reasoning doesn't make any sense considering what we know about God and how he feels about death and his creation and how much he loves them and cares for them. However, we also know how God feels about sin which is why he did what he did according to *Genesis 3:14, 9:2, Romans 8:20*. And we also know that God certainly did not create false teachers or any man to be caught and destroyed, yet that is exactly what Peter is saying about false teachers when he compares them to *"creatures of instinct meant to be caught and destroyed"*. Also Peter doesn't mention any particular species of animals either. It is my conclusion then, since the point Peter is trying to make, is the dangerousness of false teachers in leading Christians and possible converts away from the gospel and into spiritual death, he is comparing false teachers to dangerous animals that can just as easily cause physical death such as a lion or bear or other such creature, creatures that in many people's opinion are simply dangerous and a threat to human life, just as false teachers are a threat and a danger to a persons spiritual life. Remember though that these same species of animals were not always a threat to human life. It wasn't until *Genesis 9:2* that God put the fear of man upon every animal and it is also here that God said that we could use them for food.

Gen 9:2-3
2 The fear of you and the dread of you shall be upon every beast of the earth and upon every bird of the heavens, upon everything that creeps on the ground and all the fish of the sea. Into your hand they are delivered.

3 Every moving thing that lives shall be food for you. And as I gave you the green plants, I give you everything.
ESV

So why did Peter refer to such animals as "creatures of instinct meant to be caught and destroyed? Probably, because as I stated before, they are a physical threat to human life and other than being interesting creatures to watch from afar, they really served no other purpose. But does this passage say anything about them not going to heaven? Absolutely not. As a matter of fact, the time will come when there will no longer be the fear and dread upon these animals and they will live amongst us again as they did before the fall.

Isa 11:6-9
6 The wolf shall dwell with the lamb, and the leopard shall lie down with the young goat, and the calf and the lion and the fattened calf together; and a little child shall lead them.

7 The cow and the bear shall graze; their young shall lie down together; and the lion shall eat straw like the ox.

8 The nursing child shall play over the hole of the cobra, and the weaned child shall put his hand on the adder's den.

9 They shall not hurt or destroy in all my holy mountain; for the earth shall be full of the knowledge of the Lord as the waters cover the sea.
ESV

COMMONLY MISINTERPRETED VERSES

When God restores his creation to its former glory as it speaks of in *Rom 8:18-21* and makes all things new as it says in *Rev 21:5*, then obviously the curse that we live under today will be removed and the dread and fear of us humans will no longer be upon every animal as it says in *Genesis 9:2* and they will no longer be used for food.

Hos 2:18
18 And I will make for them a covenant on that day with the beasts of the field, the birds of the heavens, and the creeping things of the ground. And I will abolish the bow, the sword, and war from the land, and I will make you lie down in safety.
ESV

In *Jude 1:10* Jude is referring to the false teachers being destroyed. Does not say anything about animals being annihilated, ceasing to exist or suffering for all eternity in the fiery pits of hell.

Forever

This is a little off the subject but I thought it important to point out. Notice how the word forever is used in verse *Psalm 49:11*. This word is used many times throughout the bible to convey different messages with different meanings. Here it is used in a more temporary meaning as viewed from a worldly perspective. As we read in *1 Thess 4:16-18,* concerning the resurrection, our bodies are not going to stay in the grave permanently.

1 Thess 4:16-18
16 For the Lord himself will descend from heaven with a cry of command, with the voice of an archangel, and with the sound of the trumpet of God. And the dead in Christ will rise first.

17 Then we who are alive, who are left, will be caught up together with them in the clouds to meet the Lord in the air, and so we will always be with the Lord.

FOREVER

18 Therefore encourage one another with these words.
ESV

But as we can see from other passages it also has a more eternal or permanent meaning as in the previous verse I quoted *1 John 2:17* and the following.

Ex 15:18
18 The Lord will reign forever and ever."
ESV

Ps 23:6
6 Surely goodness and mercy shall follow me all the days of my life, and I shall dwell in the house of the Lord forever.
ESV

Ps 45:6
6 Your throne, O God, is forever and ever. The scepter of your kingdom is a scepter of uprightness;
ESV

Proof There Are Animals in Heaven Right Now

The following verses show that there are animals in heaven right now, particularly horses, and if there are horses, then why not every other creature that God created, especially the pets we loved and cared for on this earth.

2 Kings 6:17
17 Then Elisha prayed and said, "O Lord, please open his eyes that he may see." So the Lord opened the eyes of the young man, and he saw, and behold, the mountain was full of horses and chariots of fire all around Elisha.
ESV

Rev 19:11
11 Then I saw heaven opened, and behold, a white horse! The one sitting on it is called Faithful and True, and in righteousness he judges and makes war.
ESV

PROOF THERE ARE ANIMALS IN HEAVEN...

Rev 19:14
14 And the armies of heaven, arrayed in fine linen, white and pure, were following him on white horses.
ESV

The horses and chariots of fire could not be seen by the young man until Elisha prayed for the eyes of the young man to be opened. This tells me that the horses and chariots were not from this world. The only other world that I know of where these horses and chariots could have come from is heaven. Whether or not these horses were once on the earth or God created them in heaven we do not know, but they are there none the less. The same can be said of the horses mentioned in the book of revelation.

Will We Remember Our Pets? Will They Remember Us?

At this point I would like to dispel the notion some people have that when we die, we somehow no longer have consciousness or remembrance of this life or that we cease to exist. There are many verses that some people misinterpret to try to prove that when we die that the soul dies also or becomes unconscious in some way. This is just not so. They all refer to the death of the body. Some of the scripture they use are as follows.

Eccl 1:11
11 There is no remembrance of former things, nor will there be any remembrance of later things yet to be among those who come after.
ESV

Eccl 9:5
5 For the living know that they will die, but the dead

know nothing, and they have no more reward, for the memory of them is forgotten.
ESV

Eccl 1:11, Eccl 9:5 are clearly referring to the death of the body. A physical body whether it be animal or human, that is dead and decaying is obviously not going to be conscious of anything going on around it and of course it will have no more reward of things in this life such as the taste of a well cooked meal or the scent of nature on a warm summer morning or any other such reward that we now enjoy in this physical body on this earth. And obviously since there is no consciousness there will be no memory or remembrance of things past or yet to be, but look at the following passages. The following passages are proof positive that we will be conscious after the death of this physical body, we will have spiritual bodies and we will also remember who we are, where we came from and details of the life we have right now, and certainly we will remember our pets as I am confident they will remember us.

Matt 17:1-4
1 And after six days Jesus took with him Peter and James, and John his brother, and led them up a high mountain by themselves.

2 And he was transfigured before them, and his face shone like the sun, and his clothes became white as light.

3 And behold, there appeared to them Moses and Elijah, talking with him.

4 And Peter said to Jesus, "Lord, it is good that we are here. If you wish, I will make three tents here, one for you and one for Moses and one for Elijah."
ESV

According to *Deut 34:1* Moses died when he was 120 years old in the land of Moab, yet Peter and James and John saw him and recognized him as being Moses. The bible doesn't say how they recognized him since they (Peter, James and John) didn't come along till many years after Moses died. Perhaps there was a drawing of him that circulated among the people at that time. We just don't know. The same with Elijah. According to *2 King 2:11* Elijah went up by a whirlwind in to heaven, yet Peter saw him and recognized him as being Elijah. Both Elijah and Moses were talking to Jesus. If Peter recognized Elijah and Moses do you think Moses and Elijah recognized each other? Of course they did. They probably met each other in heaven since there is no evidence that they met while alive on the earth since they lived many years apart. What is also interesting is that Peter did not seem to be the least bit afraid until verse 5-7 when God appeared to them in a bright cloud.

Matt 17:5-7
5 He was still speaking when, behold, a bright cloud

overshadowed them, and a voice from the cloud said, "This is my beloved Son, with whom I am well pleased; listen to him."

6 When the disciples heard this, they fell on their faces and were terrified.

7 But Jesus came and touched them, saying, "Rise, and have no fear."
ESV

Luke 16:19-24
19 "There was a rich man who was clothed in purple and fine linen and who feasted sumptuously every day.

20 And at his gate was laid a poor man named Lazarus, covered with sores,

21 who desired to be fed with what fell from the rich man's table. Moreover, even the dogs came and licked his sores.

22 The poor man died and was carried by the angels to Abraham's side. The rich man also died and was buried,

23 and in Hades, being in torment, he lifted up his eyes and saw Abraham far off and Lazarus at his side.

24 And he called out, 'Father Abraham, have mercy on

me, and send Lazarus to dip the end of his finger in water and cool my tongue, for I am in anguish in this flame.'
ESV

The rich man here is clearly conscious as is Lazarus and in anguish. He recognizes Abraham and Lazarus. Again we don't know how he recognizes Abraham since their lives were many years apart. As I said before, possibly from some drawings that were circulating at that time. There is another observation we can make from these passages. Hell is as real as heaven and we don't want to go there.

Luke 16:25-31
25 But Abraham said, 'Child, remember that you in your lifetime received your good things, and Lazarus in like manner bad things; but now he is comforted here, and you are in anguish.

26 And besides all this, between us and you a great chasm has been fixed, in order that those who would pass from here to you may not be able, and none may cross from there to us.'

27 And he said, 'Then I beg you, father, to send him to my father's house—

28 for I have five brothers —so that he may warn them, lest they also come into this place of torment.'

WILL WE REMEMBER OUR PETS?

29 But Abraham said, 'They have Moses and the Prophets; let them hear them.'

30 And he said, 'No, father Abraham, but if someone goes to them from the dead, they will repent.'

31 He said to him, 'If they do not hear Moses and the Prophets, neither will they be convinced if someone should rise from the dead.'"
ESV

Look at verse 25. Abraham says "Child, <u>*remember*</u>", and again in verse 27 and 28 the rich man remembers his father's house and his 5 brothers. Also look at *2 Cor 5:6-8* and *Phil 1:23-24*. The writer is saying how much he would rather be with the Lord and how much better it would be to be with the Lord instead of remaining here in this body.

2 Cor 5:6-8
6 So we are always of good courage. We know that while we are at home in the body we are away from the Lord,

7 for we walk by faith, not by sight.

8 Yes, we are of good courage, and we would rather be away from the body and at home with the Lord.
ESV

WE WILL SEE OUR PETS IN HEAVEN

Phil 1:23-24
23 I am hard pressed between the two. My desire is to depart and be with Christ, for that is far better.

24 But to remain in the flesh is more necessary on your account.
ESV

Rev 6:9-11
9 When he opened the fifth seal, I saw under the altar the souls of those who had been slain for the word of God and for the witness they had borne.

10 They cried out with a loud voice, "O Sovereign Lord, holy and true, how long before you will judge and avenge our blood on those who dwell on the earth?"

11 Then they were each given a white robe and told to rest a little longer, until the number of their fellow servants and their brothers should be complete, who were to be killed as they themselves had been.
ESV

Notice verse 10. The souls of those who had been slain for the word of God are clearly conscious and crying out with a loud voice. Clearly as seen here they must have memory of their earthly lives because they are asking the Lord how much longer before he will take vengeance on the wicked who murdered them. This is just more undeniable proof that we will be conscious after our physical bodies die and we will recognize each other and have memories of this life.

Luke 23:43
43 And he said to him, "Truly, I say to you, today you will be with me in Paradise."
ESV

Here Jesus is promising the thief that he will be in Paradise, today. Keyword here is "today", not some future time, but today. Of course the thief will be conscious otherwise why would Jesus make such a promise if he wasn't going to be. Jesus could have used the word someday or not promised the thief anything if he were going to be unconscious.

2 Cor 12:1-4
1 I must go on boasting. Though there is nothing to be gained by it, I will go on to visions and revelations of the Lord.

2 I know a man in Christ who fourteen years ago was caught up to the third heaven—whether in the body or out of the body I do not know, God knows.

3 And I know that this man was caught up into paradise—whether in the body or out of the body I do not know, God knows—

WE WILL SEE OUR PETS IN HEAVEN

4 and he heard things that cannot be told, which man may not utter.
ESV

There has been much commentary on these 4 verses but I would like to focus your attention specifically on verses 2 and 3. Paul is speaking of the third heaven. This verse alone goes to show that heaven is a very real place and it is where we are going as long as we accept Jesus as our Savior. The word heaven is used throughout the bible to convey different meanings. Here Paul specifically uses the word "third heaven" so that there will be no mistake in understanding that he is talking about the dwelling place of God and that place where all the saved go when this physical body dies, and of course, where our dearly beloved pets are right now that have passed from this life. So you may be wondering, what then is the first and second heaven. The first heaven would be considered the earth's atmosphere. The second heaven would be considered outer space and then of course the third heaven is the dwelling place of God. Consider the following verses which are only a miniscule example of how the word heaven is used throughout the bible.

Gen 1:6-8
6 And God said, "Let there be an expanse in the midst of the waters, and let it separate the waters from the waters."

WILL WE REMEMBER OUR PETS?

7 And God made the expanse and separated the watersthat were under the expanse from the waters that were above the expanse. And it was so.

8 And God called the expanse Heaven. And there was evening and there was morning, the second day.
ESV

Talking about our atmosphere.

Gen 22:17
17 I will surely bless you, and I will surely multiply your offspring as the stars of heaven and as the sand that is on the seashore. And your offspring shall possess the gate of his enemies,
ESV

Here the writer is referring to outer space when he says "stars of heaven".

John 3:13
13 No one has ascended into heaven except he who descended from heaven, the Son of Man.
ESV

And again here the writer is referring to our Heavenly Father's dwelling place since he is referring to Jesus ascending into heaven. *John 3:13* has also been misinterpreted by many to try to prove that when we die that we are either unconscious or cease to exist and that no one goes to heaven when they die. But as we've seen from other passages, this is just not so. The biblical evidence that we will indeed be conscious after death, and ascend to heaven in our spiritual bodies *(as long as we're saved)* that we've seen so far is overwhelming. *John 3:13* is speaking specifically of Jesus' body being resurrected. Although Jesus was not the only body resurrected as in the case of Martha's brother, *John 11:21-23,* or the ruler's daughter, *Matthew 9:18-26* he is indeed the only one whose body died and ascended into heaven. Now Elijah on the other hand is in heaven right now but remember that he never died but was caught up to heaven by a whirlwind. *2 Kings 2:1. Heb 11:5.* Look at *John 11:25-26.* I think this verse sums it up quite well.

John 11:25-26
25 Jesus said to her, "I am the resurrection and the life. Whoever believes in me, though he die, yet shall he live,

26 and everyone who lives and believes in me shall never die. Do you believe this?"
ESV

Consider also the following verses.

Matt 22:32
32 'I am the God of Abraham, and the God of Isaac, and the God of Jacob'? He is not God of the dead, but of the living."
ESV

WILL WE REMEMBER OUR PETS?

Mark 12:27
27 He is not God of the dead, but of the living. You are quite wrong."
ESV

I think by now we have proven beyond a shadow of doubt that we will be conscious after the death of our physical bodies and that we will have memories of our life on earth. According to *Romans 14: 12,* each one of us will have to give an account of ourself to God. Obviously we will have to have memory of our lives or this simply would not be possible. But what about *Isaiah 65:17?*

Isa 65:17
17 "For behold, I create new heavens and a new earth, and the former things shall not be remembered or come into mind.
ESV

What does the writer mean then when he says that the former things shall not be remembered or come into mind? Well it certainly does not mean that we will all contract amnesia and become totally oblivious of our past as we can clearly see from the story of the rich man and Lazarus and as we saw spoken of in the book of Luke and the martyred saints spoken of in *Rev 6:9-11*. I know for a fact that there are things that have happened to you and me during this very lifetime that we have no remembrance of. Perhaps something happened to you or maybe you had an experience in your past, maybe as a child, that wasn't particularly pleasant that you have chosen to block out of your mind. I would even venture to say that you can't remember every detail of every day of your life here on earth whether you have chosen to block those memories out or not. That's not to say you couldn't choose to remember any past experiences if you wanted too and I believe it will be the same in heaven. I believe what this verse is saying basically is that heaven is going to be so glorious beyond our imagination and that we will be so occupied and enthralled by the wonders of our heavenly father's creation that any negative thoughts of this life will not even come to mind. Besides, when we're in heaven, why should we care anymore or be bothered about anything that happened to us or around us during our time on earth. I speak for myself when I say that when I'm being reunited for the first time with my pets and meeting with the other saints that have passed on before me, and taking in all the glories of heaven, that I'm not going to be thinking about the rough days I've had at work, or the time my car broke down and left me stranded somewhere or the economy, or who's going to be the next president etc, etc. I believe those are the former things that won't be remembered or come in to mind that the writer is speaking of.

WILL WE REMEMBER OUR PETS?

By now you are probably thinking this is all well and good but doesn't mention anything about animals having memories of this life. Well, that's very true it doesn't mention animals but keep in mind that the bible wasn't written for animals but for humans. Animals are sinless. They did not sin in the Garden of Eden causing God to place this earth under a curse therefore animals are not the ones in need of salvation. We are. The reason I believe animals, namely our pets, will have memories of us in this life is because of the similarities between us, but more importantly because of Gods love for us and them. Remember the insignificant little sparrow? Animals have physical bodies, we have physical bodies, animals have spirits, we have spirits, *1 Cor 15:44* animals have souls *(although not like ours because we were created in God's image),* we have souls. In my opinion then it is only logical to conclude that they will have memories of us as we will have memories of them. Think about it, you know how happy your pet is to see you when you come home after being gone all day. Just think how happy they are going to be when you finally go home to heaven and you find your pet or pets waiting for you there. Do you think God would take away their memories of you and this life on earth. Of course not. What kind of reunion would that be if when you got to heaven they didn't even know who you are. Unless of course you're not going to be there because you didn't accept Jesus as your Savior then God may take away their memories of you for their sake.

It doesn't make sense that we would remember them but they wouldn't remember us or that God would take away our memories of them since they're going to be there anyway. God made them and he loves them and saw that they were very good according to *Gen 1:25, 30* and since he never intended them or us to die to begin with, and since it was no fault of their own that man sinned and caused this curse upon the earth, *Gen 3:8-20, Rom 8:20*, they are definitely going to be there. Our father in heaven is a just God. Since God loved us so much that he sent his only son to earth do die for us sinners so that we could have eternal life, don't you think he would let his animals live again especially since they are completely innocent?

Rev 15:3
3 And they sing the song of Moses, the servant of God, and the song of the Lamb, saying, "Great and amazing are your deeds, O Lord God the Almighty! Just and true are your ways, O King of the nations!
ESV

Rev 16:7
7 And I heard the altar saying, "Yes, Lord God the Almighty, true and just are your judgments!"
ESV

WILL WE REMEMBER OUR PETS?

Hos 14:9
9 Whoever is wise, let him understand these things; whoever is discerning, let him know them; for the ways of the Lord are right, and the upright walk in them, but transgressors stumble in them.
ESV

Reality of Heaven

According to *Heb 8:5 and 9:23, 24* heaven is more real than the earth we live on.

Heb 8:1-5
1 Now the point in what we are saying is this: we have such a high priest, one who is seated at the right hand of the throne of the Majesty in heaven,

2 a minister in the holy places, in the true tent that the Lord set up, not man.

3 For every high priest is appointed to offer gifts and sacrifices; thus it is necessary for this priest also to have something to offer.

4 Now if he were on earth, he would not be a priest at all, since there are priests who offer gifts according to the law.

REALITY OF HEAVEN

5 They serve a copy and shadow of the heavenly things.
ESV

Heb 9:23-24
23 Thus it was necessary for the copies of the heavenly things to be purified with these rites, but the heavenly things themselves with better sacrifices than these.

24 For Christ has entered, not into holy places made with hands, which are copies of the true things, but into heaven itself, now to appear in the presence of God on our behalf.
ESV

According to Barnes Notes, the copy of the heavenly thing referred to in *Heb 8:5*, and the heavenly things mentioned in *Heb 9:23,24*, was the tabernacle that God commanded Moses to set up and the things inside the tabernacle. The heavenly things that they represented is the heavenly sanctuary where Jesus is right now interceding for us and where we are going, if we're saved, when we pass from this life, and it is where our pets that have died reside right now.

Hebrews 8:5 Barnes Notes

Who serve unto the example and shadow of heavenly things, as Moses was admonished of God when he was about to make the tabernacle: for, See, saith he, that thou make all things according to the pattern shewed to thee in the mount.

[Who serve unto the example] Who perform their service by the mere example and shadow of the heavenly things; or in a tabernacle, and in a mode, that is the mere emblem of the reality which exists in heaven. The reference is to the tabernacle, which was a mere "example" or "copy" of heaven. The word rendered here "example" -

hupodeigma

- means a "copy, likeness, or imitation." The tabernacle was made after a pattern which was shown to Moses; it was made so as to have some faint resemblance to the reality in heaven, and in that "copy," or "example," they were appointed to officiate. Their service, therefore, had some resemblance to that in heaven.

[And shadow] That is, in the tabernacle where they served there was a mere shadow of what was real and substantial. Compared with what is in heaven, it was what the shadow is compared with the substance. A shadow-as of a man, a house, a tree, will indicate the form, the outline, the size of the object; but it has no substance, or reality. So it was with the rites of the Jewish religion. They were designed

merely as a shadow of the substantial realities of the true religion, or to present the dim outlines of what is true and real in heaven; compare the notes on Col 2:17 Heb 10:1. The word "shadow" here -

skia

- is used in distinction from the body or reality -

sooma

- (compare Col 2:17), and also from

eikoon

- a perfect image or resemblance; see Heb 10:1.

[Of heavenly things] Of the heavenly sanctuary; of what is real and substantial in heaven. That is, there exists in heaven a reality of which the service in the Jewish sanctuary was but the outline. The reference is, undoubtedly, to the service which the Lord Jesus performs there as the great high priest of his people.

(from Barnes' Notes, Electronic Database Copyright © 1997, 2003, 2005, 2006 by Biblesoft, Inc. All rights reserved.)

Another fact to consider regarding the reality of heaven is that heaven, the third heaven, as spoken of by the apostle Paul in *2 Cor 12:2,* (our heavenly fathers dwelling place) obviously existed before this earth. It was God who created this earth and everything in it and since God is a spirit and lives in a spiritual yet tangible realm we call heaven, the only logical conclusion is that heaven is indeed a very real place and the reason I say even more real than this earth, is because it is eternal, last forever, as we've seen according to *Ex 15:18, Ps 45:6* and *2 Cor 5:1,* and the earth, that is, the works done on the earth as it says in *2 Peter 3:10* is temporal, and eventually will be destroyed. The English Standard Version actually says that the works done on the earth will be exposed whereas the King James Version uses the word destroyed. *1 John 2:17* also says that the world we're living in is passing away which I believe is also talking about the death and decay that is constantly going on around us, but as we've seen in *Eph 1:9-10* and as it says in *Rev 21:5, Rom 8:18-21* the day will come when the curse will be lifted, the earth will be made new and all things in heaven and earth will be united. Randy Alcorn in his book "Heaven" (which I highly recommend) explains it best when he says that we should stop thinking about Heaven and Earth as opposites and instead view them as overlapping circles that share certain commonalities. One of those commonalities being the presence of animals, particularly our pets. He also points out that these verses in Hebrews suggest that God created Earth in the image of Heaven, just as he created mankind in his image. The fact that Jesus is living there right now in his physical resurrected body and Elijah in his physical body, also suggest that even though we consider Heaven as a spiritual place, it is also very physical in nature and containing physical objects such as plants, animals, and various terrain similar to what we're familiar with on this earth and what we read about in Genesis regarding the Garden of Eden, only much better! Even though Moses was not resurrected, he was still able to be seen and recognized by Peter James and John which is also indication that even our spiritual bodies must have some physical properties or he wouldn't have been able to be seen.

2 Peter 3:10
10 But the day of the Lord will come like a thief, and then the heavens will pass away with a roar, and the heavenly bodies will be burned up and dissolved, and the earth and the works that are done on it will be exposed.
ESV

Adam Clarks Commentary puts it this way.

1 John 2:17
And the world passeth away, and the lust thereof: but he that doeth the will of God abideth for ever.

WE WILL SEE OUR PETS IN HEAVEN

[The world passeth away] All these things are continually fading and perishing; and the very state in which they are possessed is changing perpetually; and the earth and its works will be shortly burnt up.

[And the lust thereof] The men of this world, their vain pursuits, and delusive pleasures, as passing away in their successive generations, and their very memory perishes; but he that doeth the will of God-that seeks the pleasure, profit, and honour that comes from above, shall abide forever, always happy through time and eternity, because God, the unchangeable source of felicity, is his portion.

(from Adam Clarke's Commentary, Electronic Database. Copyright © 1996, 2003, 2005, 2006 by Biblesoft, Inc. All rights reserved.)

2 Cor 5:1 also speaks of our earthly home being destroyed, and that we have a permanent home that our Heavenly Father has made for us that is eternal.

2 Cor 5:1
5 For we know that if the tent, which is our earthly home, is destroyed, we have a building from God, a house not made with hands, eternal in the heavens.
ESV

The Good News

That dog, cat, horse, bunny, lamb, pig or whatever it was that you had as a pet that you loved so much, that you had to say goodbye to when it passed away, is alive and well in it's spiritual body, without any of the infirmities that plagued it in this life. It's in heaven right now waiting for you. Remember that God created them, they are his, he loves them and cares for them and never intended for them to die in the beginning as we have seen throughout scripture. Remember the Sparrow. Not one of them is forgotten or falls to the ground apart from our heavenly father as we've seen in *Matt 10:29*, *Luke 12:6*. But more importantly our heavenly father loves us and he knows how much our pets mean to us. The title of this book is "We Will See Our Pets In Heaven". This is only true if you're going to be there too. The big question now is, are you going to be there? There is only one way to get to heaven and that is through Jesus Christ

Do You Know What It Takes to Get to Heaven

Do you know what it takes to get there? Do you know what you have to do to be saved? You must believe that Jesus is Lord, he came to earth and died for us, *John 3:16* and it is only through him that we have salvation. *John 14:6-7*

You must have faith and believe that Jesus died for you and shed his blood to pay the penalty for our sins and it is by grace through faith that we are saved according to *Eph 2: 8-10*. We are also instructed to be baptized as it says in *Mark 16:16, John 3:5, Acts 2:38*.

Mark 16:16
16 Whoever believes and is baptized will be saved, but whoever does not believe will be condemned.
ESV

DO YOU KNOW WHAT IT TAKES...

John 3:5
5 Jesus answered, "Truly, truly, I say to you, unless one is born of water and the Spirit, he cannot enter the kingdom of God.
ESV

Acts 2:38
38 And Peter said to them, "Repent and be baptized every one of you in the name of Jesus Christ for the forgiveness of your sins, and you will receive the gift of the Holy Spirit
ESV

Rom 3:23-25
23 for all have sinned and fall short of the glory of God,

24 and are justified by his grace as a gift, through the redemption that is in Christ Jesus,

25 whom God put forward as a propitiation by his blood, to be received by faith.
ESV

John 3:16
16 "For God so loved the world, that he gave his only Son, that whoever believes in him should not perish but have eternal life
ESV

WE WILL SEE OUR PETS IN HEAVEN

John 14:6
6 Jesus said to him, "I am the way, and the truth, and the life. No one comes to the Father except through me.
ESV

Heb 11:6
6 And without faith it is impossible to please him, for whoever would draw near to God must believe that he exists and that he rewards those who seek him.
ESV

Eph 2:8-10
8 For by grace you have been saved through faith. And this is not your own doing; it is the gift of God,

9 not a result of works, so that no one may boast.

10 For we are his workmanship, created in Christ Jesus for good works, which God prepared beforehand, that we should walk in them.
ESV

Receive Jesus as your savior today. Find a good bible based church. If you don't have a bible I highly recommend the English Standard Version. Read it. Study it. See what our heavenly father requires of us.

2 Tim 2:15
15 Do your best to present yourself to God as one approved,

DO YOU KNOW WHAT IT TAKES...

a worker who has no need to be ashamed, rightly handling the word of truth.
ESV

Rom 10:13
13 For "everyone who calls on the name of the Lord will be saved."
ESV

Ps 84:3
*3 Even the sparrow finds a home,
and the swallow a nest for herself,
where she may lay her young,
at your altars, O Lord of hosts,
my King and my God.
ESV*

Reading List

The following is a list of books that I highly recommend if you desire a deeper understanding and insight into what heaven will be like and God's plan for his animals.

Heaven by Randy Alcorn

Will I See Him Again by Tom Waldron

There Is Eternal Life for Animals by Niki Behrikis Shanahan

Who Says Animals Go to Heaven by Niki Behrikis Shanahan

Cold Noses at the Pearly Gates by Gary Kurz

Cold Noses II Examining More Evidence by Gary Kurz

God of Me Too by Gary Kurz

Will I See Fido in Heaven by Mary Buddemeyer-Porter

Animal, Immortal Beings by Mary Buddemeyer-Porter

Animals in Heaven: Fantasy or Reality? by Arch Stanton

Will I See My Dog in Heaven? by Jack Wintz

90 Minutes in Heaven by Don Piper

Heaven Is for Real by Todd Burpo

Proof of Heaven by Eben Alexander, MD